HOW

A comprehensive roof framing guidebook introducing the art of building and designing rafters effectively for beginners

ROBERTSON BROCK

Table of Contents

CHAPTER ONE 5

  INTRODUCTION 5

  HISTORY OF RAFTERS 6

  IMPORTANCE OF RAFTERS 8

  RAFTER BUILDING TECHNIQUES 10

  TYPES OF RAFTERS 15

  PARTS OF A RAFTER 18

  COMMON RAFTERS 22

  HIP RAFTERS 26

  JACK RAFTERS 29

  COLLAR TIES 33

  VALLEY RAFTERS 37

  STRUCTURAL INSULATED PANELS (SIPS) 41

  TOOLS AND MATERIALS NEEDED TO BUILD RAFTERS 45

CHAPTER TWO 49

  BUILDING RAFTERS USING ONLINE CALCULATORS 49

  IMPORTANCE OF USING ONLINE CALCULATORS AND EXAMPLES 52

  HOW TO BUILD RAFTERS 55

DETERMINING THE SIZE AND DESIGN OF THE ROOF 59

CUTTING THE RAFTERS 63

NOTCHING THE RAFTERS 66

INSTALLING HANGERS OR BRACKETS...........69

INSTALLING THE RIDGE BEAM 73

INSTALLING THE ROOFING UNDERLAYMENT 76

INSTALLING THE ROOFING...........................80

INSTALLING COLLAR TIES 84

CHAPTER THREE 88

SIMPLE GUIDE TO BUILDING A GABLE ROOF RAFTER FOR A SHED......................................88

HOW TO MAKE FRAME RAFTERS FOR A BARN 93

GENERAL TECHNIQUE FOR SPACING RAFTERS 97

HOW TO EFFICIENTLY CUT RIDGE BOARD, BIRDMOUTH, AND TAIL END WHILE BUILDING RAFTERS 102

HOW TO INSTALL TRUSS RAFTERS 106

COMMON MISTAKES TO AVOID WHILE
BUILDING RAFTERS AND HOW TO
TROUBLESHOOT THEM 109

FAQ 113

CONCLUSION.. 117

THE END 120

CHAPTER ONE

INTRODUCTION

Rafters are horizontal beams that go from a roof's ridge (or peak) to a building's eaves (or margins). They are used to support the roof deck (which is normally built of plywood or planks) and to transmit the weight of the roof and snow loads to the building's walls and foundation. Rafters are an important component of a building's construction because they contribute to the overall strength and stability of the roof.

while minimizing the use of materials.

IMPORTANCE OF RAFTERS

Rafters are critical to a building's overall structural integrity and stability. Rafters are important for a variety of reasons, including:

Roof Support: Rafters support the roof deck and transmit the weight of the roof, snow loads, and other pressures to the building's walls and base.

Rafters contribute to the stability and strength of the roof, keeping it from collapsing and giving shelter from the weather.

Rafters that are properly placed can assist increase a building's energy efficiency by providing insulation and ventilation.

Aesthetics: Rafters may contribute significantly to a building's aesthetic attractiveness. Rafters were frequently exposed and used as ornamental components in a traditional buildings.

Rafters can serve to extend the life of a structure by providing stable and long-lasting support for the roof when built of robust materials.

In conclusion, rafters are an essential component of every structure, contributing to its safety, stability, and energy efficiency.

RAFTER BUILDING TECHNIQUES

There are several techniques for building roof rafters, including:

Traditional Cut Rafters: This technique involves cutting each rafter individually to size and installing them one by one. It is a traditional method that is still widely used today and provides a high degree of accuracy and control.

Engineered Rafters: Engineered rafters are pre-manufactured roof framing members that are designed to specific specifications and standards. They are engineered to provide a high degree of strength and stability and are often used in larger or more complex roof designs.

Truss Systems: Truss systems are pre-manufactured roof framing members that are made up of interconnected triangles. They provide a high degree of strength and stability and are often used in large or complex roof designs.

Prefabricated Panels: Prefabricated panels are pre-manufactured roof framing members that are made up of interconnected rafters and purlins. They provide a high degree of strength and stability and are often used in large or complex roof designs.

Stick-Built: Stick-built roof framing involves building the roof structure on site, using traditional cut rafters, ridge beams, collar ties, and other components. This method provides a high degree of control and flexibility and is often used in custom or unique roof designs.

Structural Insulated Panels (SIPs): SIPs are pre-manufactured panels that consist of a foam insulation core sandwiched between two layers of oriented strand board (OSB). They provide both insulation and structural support and are a popular option for energy-efficient homes.

Note: The most appropriate rafter building technique will depend on the size and design of the roof, the type of roofing material being used, and the requirements of local building codes and standards. It is recommended to consult with a professional contractor or roofing expert to determine the best technique for your specific roof design.

TYPES OF RAFTERS

There are several types of rafters used in construction, each with its own set of characteristics and uses:

Common Rafters: These are the most basic type of rafters and are used in simple roof designs. They run from the ridge of the roof to the eaves and are spaced evenly apart to support the roof deck.

Hip Rafters: Hip rafters are used in roofs with hipped ends (or angled ends) and run from the ridge of the roof to the corners of the building. They provide additional support to the roof at these critical points.

Jack Rafters: Jack rafters are smaller rafters used in conjunction with common or hip rafters to provide additional support in areas where the roof slope changes.

Valley Rafters: Valley rafters are used in roofs with valleys (or low points) and run from the ridge of the roof to the valleys. They provide additional support to the roof in these areas.

Collar Ties: Collar ties are short pieces of lumber that run between opposite rafters near the ridge of the roof. They help to prevent the rafters from spreading apart and ensure stability and strength in the roof.

Structural Insulated Panels (SIPs): SIPs are prefabricated panels made from foam insulation and either OSB or plywood that serve as both the roof deck and the rafters. They offer a high level of insulation and are becoming increasingly popular in green buildings.

The type of rafter used in a building depends on the roof design, the materials used, and the local building codes. The right choice of rafter type can help ensure the stability, strength, and energy efficiency of a building for years to come.

PARTS OF A RAFTER

A rafter is a structural component of a building and typically consists of several parts:

Plates: The plates are the bottom members of the rafters and rest on the walls of the building. They serve as the point of connection between the rafters and the building structure.

Ridge: The ridge is the highest point of the roof and the rafters meet at the ridge to form the peak of the roof.

Tail: The tail is the bottom end of the rafter and extends from the plate to the eaves.

Seat Cut: The seat cut is a notched area in the plate where the rafter sits. This provides a secure and stable connection between the rafter and the plate.

Bird's Mouth: The bird's mouth is a V-shaped cutout in the tail of the rafter that allows it to fit snugly against the top plate of the wall.

Heel: The heel is the point where the ridge and the tail of the rafter intersect.

Crown Cut: The crown cut is a decorative cut at the top of the rafter near the ridge that enhances the aesthetic appeal of the roof.

Fly Rafter: The fly rafter is a short piece of lumber used to connect the tail of the rafter to the roof deck.

These are the basic parts of a rafter, and the specific components used in a building will depend on the design, materials, and local building codes. Understanding the different parts of a rafter can help ensure that the roof of a building is properly constructed and can provide reliable and long-lasting support.

COMMON RAFTERS

Common rafters are a type of rafter used in simple roof designs. They are typically made from dimensional lumber, such as 2x6, 2x8, or 2x10, and run from the ridge of the roof to the eaves. Some key features and characteristics of common rafters include:

Spacing: Common rafters are spaced evenly apart to provide

support for the roof deck. The spacing of the rafters is determined by the type of roofing material used, the weight of the roof, and local building codes.

Length: The length of the common rafters is determined by the span of the roof and the height of the walls. Longer rafters are typically used in wider roof spans to provide the necessary support.

Load-Bearing Capacity: Common rafters are designed to carry the weight of the roof, including the roofing material, snow loads, and other forces. They must be strong enough to support these loads and prevent the roof from collapsing.

Installation: Common rafters are typically installed before the roof deck and must be properly attached to the ridge and the wall plates. They must be securely fastened to ensure stability and prevent movement.

Ventilation: Common rafters can also play a role in roof ventilation by providing a space for air to circulate and help remove moisture.

In conclusion, common rafters are a fundamental component of simple roof designs and play an important role in ensuring the stability and strength of the roof. Proper installation and maintenance of the common rafters can help extend the life of a building and protect it from the elements.

HIP RAFTERS

Hip rafters are a type of rafter used in roof designs that have sloping sides, such as a gable or hipped roof. They differ from common rafters in that they form the intersection of two sloping sides of the roof. Some key features and characteristics of hip rafters include:

Complex Shape: Hip rafters have a more complex shape than common rafters and require careful cutting and fitting to ensure a tight, secure connection. They must be cut to match the angle of the roof slope and the length of the hip.

Load-Bearing Capacity: Hip rafters are designed to carry the weight of the roof, including the roofing material, snow loads, and other forces. They must be strong enough to support these loads and prevent the roof from collapsing.

Support: Hip rafters are typically installed in pairs and provide support for the ridge and the other rafters on the roof. They help to transfer the load of the roof to the walls of the building.

Installation: Hip rafters are typically installed before the roof deck and must be properly attached to the ridge, the walls, and the other rafters in the roof. They must be securely fastened to ensure stability and prevent movement.

Ventilation: Hip rafters can also play a role in roof ventilation by providing a space for air to circulate and help remove moisture.

In conclusion, hip rafters are an important component of roof designs that have sloping sides. They play a crucial role in ensuring the stability and strength of the roof and must be installed properly to provide reliable support. Proper installation and maintenance of the hip rafters can help extend the life of a building and protect it from the elements.

JACK RAFTERS

Jack rafters are a type of roof rafter that is shorter in length than common rafters and are used in the construction of roofs with a gable or hip design. They play an important role in supporting the roof and transferring the load to the walls of the building. Some key features and characteristics of jack rafters include:

Size: Jack rafters are typically shorter in length than common rafters and are used to fill in the space between the ridge and the wall plates. They are also used to support the end of the ridge board.

Load-Bearing: Jack rafters are designed to carry the weight of the roof, including the roofing material, snow loads, and other forces. They must be strong enough to support these loads and prevent the roof from collapsing.

Support: Jack rafters provide support for the ridge and other rafters on the roof. They help to transfer the load of the roof to the walls of the building and provide stability to the roof structure.

Installation: Jack rafters are typically installed before the roof deck and must be properly attached to the ridge, the walls, and the other rafters in the roof. They must be securely fastened to ensure stability and prevent movement.

Ventilation: Jack rafters can also play a role in roof ventilation by providing a space for air to circulate and help remove moisture.

In conclusion, jack rafters are an important component of roof designs with a gable or hip design. They play a crucial role in ensuring the stability and strength of the roof and must be installed properly to provide reliable support. Proper installation and maintenance of the jack rafters can help extend the life of a building and protect it from the elements.

COLLAR TIES

Collar ties are structural components used in roof construction to help prevent the rafters from spreading apart and to provide additional stability to the roof. Some key features and characteristics of collar ties include:

Function: Collar ties are installed in the attic space and run perpendicular to the rafters. They help to keep the rafters from spreading apart and provide additional support to the roof structure. This helps to ensure the stability of the roof and prevent it from collapsing.

Installation: Collar ties are typically installed near the ridge of the roof, and are fastened to the rafters. They can be made of wood or metal and must be securely fastened to provide reliable support.

Height: The height of the collar ties is an important consideration. They should be installed at a sufficient height to provide adequate support to the roof structure, while still allowing adequate headroom in the attic space.

Design: Collar ties are designed to be strong and durable. They must be able to withstand the weight of the roof and the forces generated by wind and other weather conditions.

Building Codes: Collar ties are often required by building codes to help ensure the stability and safety of the roof structure. Building codes specify the size, spacing, and other design requirements for collar ties.

In conclusion, collar ties are an important component of roof construction and play a crucial role in ensuring the stability of the roof. Proper installation and maintenance of the collar ties can help extend the life of a building and protect it from the elements. It is recommended to consult a professional builder or architect to ensure that the collar ties are installed correctly and meet local building codes.

VALLEY RAFTERS

Valley rafters are roofing components that are used in the construction of roofs that have a valley design, which is an indentation in the roof where two sloping sides meet. Valley rafters play an important role in ensuring the stability of the roof and transferring the load to the walls of the building. Some key features and characteristics of valley rafters include:

Design: Valley rafters are typically shaped like a triangle and are installed in the valley of the roof. They are designed to provide additional support to the roof structure and help distribute the load of the roof to the walls of the building.

Load-Bearing: Valley rafters are designed to carry the weight of the roof, including the roofing material, snow loads, and other forces. They must be strong enough to support these loads and prevent the roof from collapsing.

Size: The size of the valley rafters depends on the size and design of the roof. They must be large enough to provide adequate support to the roof structure, while still allowing adequate headroom in the attic space.

Installation: Valley rafters are typically installed before the roof deck and must be properly attached to the ridge, the walls, and the other rafters in the roof.

They must be securely fastened to ensure stability and prevent movement.

Ventilation: Valley rafters can also play a role in roof ventilation by providing a space for air to circulate and help remove moisture.

In conclusion, valley rafters are an important component of roofs with a valley design. They play a crucial role in ensuring the stability and strength of the roof and must be installed properly to provide reliable support. Proper installation and maintenance of the valley rafters can help extend the life of a building and protect it from the elements.

STRUCTURAL INSULATED PANELS (SIPS)

Structural Insulated Panels (SIPs) are a type of building material that combines insulation and structural elements into one component. They are commonly used in residential and commercial construction as a cost-effective and energy-efficient alternative to traditional building methods. Some key features and characteristics of SIPs include:

Design: SIPs are made of a foam insulation core sandwiched between two layers of oriented strand board (OSB). The foam core provides insulation, while the OSB layers provide structural strength.

Energy Efficiency: The foam insulation in SIPs helps to reduce energy loss through the walls and roof of a building, making it more energy-efficient and reducing heating and cooling costs.

Speed of Construction: SIPs can be cut to size and installed quickly, reducing the time required for construction and minimizing the need for additional materials such as insulation and drywall.

Strength and Durability: SIPs provide structural support and stability to a building, and are resistant to fire, moisture, and pests.

Cost-effectiveness: SIPs can be a cost-effective alternative to traditional building methods, as they reduce the need for additional materials and labor, and can help reduce energy costs over the life of the building.

Building Codes: SIPs must meet local building codes and standards, which specify the minimum thickness, fire rating, and other requirements for the insulation and structural components.

In conclusion, Structural Insulated Panels (SIPs) are versatile and energy-efficient building materials that can be used in a variety of residential and commercial construction applications. They provide strong, durable, and energy-efficient buildings and can be a cost-effective alternative to traditional building methods. It is recommended to consult with a professional builder or engineer to ensure that SIPs are installed correctly and meet local building codes.

TOOLS AND MATERIALS NEEDED TO BUILD RAFTERS

To build rafters, you will need the following tools and materials:

Tools:

- Measuring tape
- Square
- Framing hammer
- Circular saw
- Power drill
- Safety goggles
- Hearing protection
- Carpenter's level
- Chalk line
- Extension ladder

Materials:

- Lumber (2x6 or 2x8)
- Roofing nails
- Hangers or brackets

- Joist hangers
- Plywood
- Collar ties (if required)
- Ridge beam (if required)
- Roofing underlayment
- Roofing shingles or metal roofing panels

Note: The specific materials and tools required will depend on the size and design of the roof and the type of rafters being installed.

It is important to always use proper safety equipment and follow local building codes when installing rafters. Additionally, it is recommended to consult with a professional builder or engineer to ensure that the rafters are installed correctly and meet all required building codes and standards.

CHAPTER TWO

BUILDING RAFTERS USING ONLINE CALCULATORS

Online rafters calculators may be a useful tool for individuals who are constructing a roof. The following are the steps for creating rafters with online calculators:

Establish the roof specifications: The span length, ridge height, and roof pitch are all included.

Select the type of roof: This might be a gable, hip, or shed roof.

Pick your wood: the roof's weight is affected by the type of wood chosen, thus the size of the rafters must be calculated accordingly.

To use the calculator, provide the following information about the roof: Most online calculators will ask for the roof span length, ridge height, roof pitch, and wood type.

Use the calculator findings as follows: The calculator will calculate the rafter size required, the length of the ridge board, and the length of the birdsmouth cut.

rafters should be cut and installed: Cut and install the rafters according to the specifications using the calculator results.

It is crucial to remember that, while online rafter calculators might be helpful, they should only be used as a starting point. Before beginning any building job, it is usually essential to contact a skilled contractor or engineer.

IMPORTANCE OF USING ONLINE CALCULATORS AND EXAMPLES

Using online rafter calculators may be beneficial in a variety of ways:

Saves time: When compared to manual calculations, online calculators can rapidly offer the essential parameters for the rafters.

Reduces the danger of calculation errors: Online calculators can lessen the risk of calculation errors, which can be costly in terms of materials and time.

Some online calculators give graphic representations of the roof and rafters, which can assist in understanding and visualizing the job.

Takes into account particular conditions: Some online calculators take into account particular variables like wind loads and snow loads, which might affect the size of the rafters required.

Online calculators are conveniently available from any device with an internet connection, making them ideal for on-the-go use.

The Roof Rafter Calculator by ConstructionCalc is an example of an online rafter calculator. It specifies the appropriate dimensions, length, and birdsmouth cut for common, hip, valley, and jack rafters. The calculator provides the answers once the user enters the span length, ridge height, roof pitch, and kind of wood.

HOW TO BUILD RAFTERS

Building rafters can be a complex and challenging task that requires specialized skills, tools, and experience. However, a general step-by-step guide for building common rafters is as follows:

Determine the size and design of the roof: Before building the rafters, you will need to determine the size and design of the roof, including the span, pitch, and load requirements.

Cut the rafters: Cut the rafters to length based on the design of the roof. The rafters should be cut to the proper length, slope, and angle.

Notch the rafters: Notch the rafters at the top and bottom to fit over the ridge beam and into the wall plates.

Install hangers or brackets: Install hangers or brackets at the bottom of the rafters to support them.

Install the ridge beam: If required, install the ridge beam along the top of the roof. The rafters will rest on the ridge beam and be secured to it.

Install the roofing underlayment: Install the roofing underlayment on top of the rafters to provide a base for the roofing shingles or metal roofing panels.

Install the roofing: Install the roofing shingles or metal roofing panels on top of the roofing underlayment.

Install collar ties: If required, install collar ties to provide additional support and stability to the roof structure.

Note: The specific steps required for building rafters will depend on the size and design of the roof, the type of rafters being installed, and local building codes and standards.

It is important to always use proper safety equipment and follow local building codes when installing rafters. Additionally, it is recommended to consult with a professional builder or engineer to ensure that the rafters are installed correctly and meet all required building codes and standards.

DETERMINING THE SIZE AND DESIGN OF THE ROOF

Determining the size and design of the roof is a crucial step in building rafters. The size and design of the roof will determine the size, length, slope, and angle of the rafters, as well as the load-bearing capacity and stability of the roof structure. The following are some of the key factors to consider when determining the size and design of the roof:

Roof span: The roof span is the distance between the outside walls of the building. This will determine the length of the rafters and the size of the ridge beam if required.

Roof pitch: The roof pitch is the slope of the roof, expressed as the ratio of the height of the roof to the span. The roof pitch will determine the height and slope of the rafters.

Load requirements: The load requirements will determine the size and strength of the rafters and the roof structure. The load requirements will include the weight of the roofing materials, snow, and wind loads.

Building codes and standards: Building codes and standards will determine the minimum size and strength of the rafters and the roof structure. It is important to follow local building codes and standards to ensure the safety and stability of the roof.

Climate: Climate will also impact the design of the roof, including the type of roofing materials, the ventilation requirements, and the insulation requirements.

Architectural style: The architectural style of the building will also impact the design of the roof, including the type of roofing materials, the pitch, and the style of the rafters.

Note: The specific design requirements will depend on the size and complexity of the roof and the local building codes and standards. It is recommended to consult with a professional builder or engineer to determine the size and design of the roof and to ensure that the roof structure meets all required building codes and standards.

CUTTING THE RAFTERS

Cutting the rafters is an important step in building rafters, and requires precise measurements, accuracy, and experience. The following are some general steps for cutting the rafters:

Measure the length of the rafters: Measure the length of the rafters based on the design of the roof, including the span and pitch of the roof. The length of the rafters will determine the height of the roof.

Cut the top and bottom of the rafters: Cut the top and bottom of the rafters to the correct slope and angle based on the pitch of the roof. The top of the rafters will rest on the ridge beam, and the bottom of the rafters will fit into the wall plates.

Cut the notches: Cut notches into the top and bottom of the rafters to fit over the ridge beam and into the wall plates.

Make any additional cuts: Make any additional cuts, such as bird's mouth cuts, if required.

Note: The specific steps for cutting the rafters will depend on the size and design of the roof and the type of rafters being installed. It is recommended to use a saw or cutting tool that is appropriate for the size and type of the rafters and to follow proper safety procedures when cutting the rafters.

Additionally, it is important to check and double-check the measurements and cuts of the rafters to ensure that they are accurate and meet the requirements of the roof design and building codes and standards.

NOTCHING THE RAFTERS

Notching the rafters is the process of cutting out spaces or recesses at the top and bottom of the rafters to accommodate the ridge beam and the wall plates. Notching the rafters is a critical step in building a roof structure and requires precise measurements, accuracy, and experience. The following are some general steps for notching the rafters:

Measure the ridge beam: Measure the ridge beam to determine the size and spacing of the notches at the top of the rafters.

Mark the notches: Mark the notches at the top of the rafters using a framing square and a pencil.

Cut the notches: Cut out the notches using a saw or cutting tool that is appropriate for the size and type of the rafters.

Repeat the process for the bottom of the rafters: Repeat the process of measuring, marking, and cutting the notches for the bottom of the rafters, to fit into the wall plates.

Check the notches: Check the notches to ensure that they are the correct size and shape to fit over the ridge beam and into the wall plates.

Note: The specific steps for notching the rafters will depend on the size and design of the roof and the type of rafters being installed. It is important to follow proper safety procedures when cutting the notches and to check and double-check the measurements and cuts of the notches to ensure that they are accurate and meet the requirements of the roof design and building codes and standards.

INSTALLING HANGERS OR BRACKETS

Installing hangers or brackets is the process of attaching a support system to the bottom of the rafters to hold them in place and transfer the weight of the roof to the wall plates or other structural support. Hangers or brackets are typically made of metal, such as steel or aluminum, and are attached to the bottom of the rafters using nails or screws. The following are some general steps for installing hangers or brackets:

Measure the spacing: Measure the spacing between the rafters to determine the placement of the hangers or brackets.

Cut the hangers or brackets: Cut the hangers or brackets to the correct length based on the spacing between the rafters.

Attach the hangers or brackets: Attach the hangers or brackets to the bottom of the rafters using nails or screws.

Secure the hangers or brackets: Secure the hangers or brackets in place to ensure that they are properly installed and can support the weight of the roof.

Repeat the process: Repeat the process of measuring, cutting, attaching, and securing the hangers or brackets for each of the rafters.

Note: The specific steps for installing hangers or brackets will depend on the size and design of the roof and the type of hangers or brackets being used. It is recommended to follow the manufacturer's instructions and to check and double-check the placement and installation of the hangers or brackets to ensure that they meet the requirements of the roof design and building codes and standards.

INSTALLING THE RIDGE BEAM

Installing the ridge beam is the process of placing the central support structure of the roof, which runs along the peak of the roof. The ridge beam is usually made of strong and durable materials, such as lumber, steel, or engineered lumber. The following are some general steps for installing the ridge beam:

Measure the placement: Measure the placement of the ridge beam, making sure that it is centered on the top of the wall plates and evenly spaced between the two sides of the roof.

Cut the ridge beam: Cut the ridge beam to the correct length based on the measurement of the placement.

Install the ridge beam: Install the ridge beam by placing it on top of the wall plates and securing it in place using nails or screws.

Install hangers: Install hangers, which are brackets that attach to the bottom of the ridge beam, on each of the rafters to support the ridge beam.

Check the ridge beam: Check the ridge beam to ensure that it is level, straight, and securely installed, and that the hangers are properly attached and able to support the weight of the roof.

Note: The specific steps for installing the ridge beam will depend on the size and design of the roof and the type of ridge beam being used. It is recommended to follow proper safety procedures and to check and double-check the placement, installation, and stability of the ridge beam to ensure that it meets the requirements of the roof design and building codes and standards.

INSTALLING THE ROOFING UNDERLAYMENT

Installing the roofing underlayment is the process of placing a protective layer between the roof deck and the roofing material to provide additional insulation and weather protection. The roofing underlayment is typically made of synthetic materials, such as asphalt-saturated felt, that are designed to be durable and water-resistant. The following are some general steps for installing the roofing underlayment:

Prepare the roof deck: Prepare the roof deck by cleaning it of any debris and ensuring that it is free of any damage or defects that could compromise the installation of the roofing underlayment.

Install the underlayment: Roll out the roofing underlayment and place it on top of the roof deck, starting from the bottom edge of the roof and working your way up.

Secure the underlayment: Secure the underlayment in place using roofing nails or staples, making sure to overlap the seams of each sheet by at least 6 inches and to properly fasten it to the roof deck.

Install any necessary flashing: Install any necessary flashing, such as around roof penetrations, to ensure that the underlayment is properly sealed and protected.

Inspect the underlayment: Inspect the underlayment to ensure that it is properly installed and free of any defects or damage that could compromise its effectiveness.

Note: The specific steps for installing the roofing underlayment will depend on the size and design of the roof, the type of underlayment being used, and the requirements of local building codes and standards. It is recommended to follow the manufacturer's instructions and to check and double-check the installation of the underlayment to ensure that it meets the requirements of the roof design and provides adequate protection.

INSTALLING THE ROOFING

Installing the roofing is the process of placing the final layer of material that provides protection from the elements and enhances the appearance of the roof. The roofing material can be made of various materials, such as asphalt shingles, metal panels, clay tiles, or slate tiles. The following are some general steps for installing the roofing:

Prepare the roof deck: Prepare the roof deck by cleaning it of any debris and ensuring that it is free of any damage or defects that could compromise the installation of the roofing material.

Install the starter course: Install the starter course, which is the first row of roofing material, along the bottom edge of the roof. The starter course should be properly fastened to the roof deck and should have the correct overlap with the roofing underlayment.

Install the main roofing: Install the main roofing by placing the roofing material on top of the starter course and working your way up the roof. The roofing material should be properly fastened to the roof deck and should have the correct overlap and alignment with the previous row of roofing material.

Install any necessary flashings: Install any necessary flashings, such as around roof penetrations, to ensure that the roofing material is properly sealed and protected.

Inspect the roofing: Inspect the roofing to ensure that it is properly installed and free of any defects or damage that could compromise its effectiveness.

Note: The specific steps for installing the roofing will depend on the size and design of the roof, the type of roofing material being used, and the requirements of local building codes and standards. It is recommended to follow the manufacturer's instructions and to check and double-check the installation of the roofing to ensure that it meets the requirements of the roof design and provides adequate protection from the elements.

INSTALLING COLLAR TIES

Installing collar ties is a process of securing the rafters to prevent the roof from spreading apart or sagging. Collar ties are usually installed near the ridge of the roof and are typically made of wood. The following are the general steps for installing collar ties:

Determine the location of the collar ties: The location of the collar ties will depend on the design of the roof and the load it will bear. Collar ties should be installed at a distance from the ridge equal to one-third to one-half the span of the rafters.

Cut the collar ties: Cut the collar ties to the correct length and shape. The collar ties should fit snugly between the rafters and should be strong enough to provide adequate support to the roof.

Install the collar ties: Install the collar ties by nailing or screwing them to the top of the rafters. The collar ties should be securely fastened to the rafters and should not be obstructed by any other roofing components or materials.

Check the installation: Check the installation of the collar ties to ensure that they are properly installed and secure.

Note: The specific steps for installing collar ties will depend on the size and design of the roof, the type of roofing material being used, and the requirements of local building codes and standards. It is recommended to follow the manufacturer's instructions and to check and double-check the installation of the collar ties to ensure that they provide adequate support to the roof and meet the requirements of the roof design.

CHAPTER THREE

SIMPLE GUIDE TO BUILDING A GABLE ROOF RAFTER FOR A SHED

A gable roof rafter is a type of roofing rafter that is used in construction to support the roof structure of a gable roof. A gable roof is a roof that has two sloping sides that meet at the ridge or peak of the roof, forming a triangle shape. The gable roof rafters run from the ridge beam at the peak of the roof down to the wall plate at the top of the walls, forming the triangle shape of the gable. The gable roof rafters are typically made from lumber, such as 2x6 or 2x8, and are designed to carry the weight of the roof and any additional loads, such as snow or wind, down to the walls and foundations. They are usually spaced evenly along the ridge beam and are typically notched at the wall plate to fit snugly against the top of the walls.

Building a rafter is a complex task that requires a solid understanding of construction principles and techniques. The following is a step-by-step example of building a simple gable roof rafter for a 10' x 12' shed:

Determine the size and spacing of the rafters: Based on the design of the roof and the size of the shed, determine the size of the rafters and the spacing between them. For this example, 2x6 rafters spaced 16 inches in the center are used.

Cut the ridge board: Cut a 2x6 ridge board to the correct length, which is the length of the shed plus the overhang on both ends.

Cut the bird's mouth: Cut the bird's mouth in the rafters, which is a notch at the bottom of the rafter where it rests on the top plate of the wall. The bird's mouth should be cut so that the rafter sits level on the top plate and is flush with the wall.

Cut the tail end: Cut the tail end of the rafter, which is the end that extends past the wall. The tail end should be cut to the correct length, which is determined by the overhang of the roof and the slope of the roof.

Install the ridge board: Install the ridge board by nailing or screwing it to the top plate of the wall, making sure that it is level and centered on the shed.

Install the rafters: Install the rafters by nailing or screwing them to the ridge board and the top plate of the wall. Make sure that the rafters are spaced correctly and are level.

Install the collar ties: If necessary, install the collar ties by nailing or screwing them to the tops of the rafters, near the ridge.

Check the installation: Check the installation of the rafters, ridge board, and collar ties to ensure that they are properly installed and secure.

HOW TO MAKE FRAME RAFTERS FOR A BARN

Making frame rafters for a barn typically involves the following steps:

Determine the size of the barn and the design of the roof. This will give you an idea of how many rafters you need and what the spacing between the rafters should be.

Cut the lumber to size. The most common wood used for barn rafters is 2x6 or 2x8 lumber.

Mark the cut lines on the lumber. Use a framing square to ensure that the cuts are straight and accurate.

Cut the notches for the rafters. You can either use a handsaw or a circular saw with a guide to making the cuts.

Join the rafters using a scarf joint. You can use a biscuit cutter or a plate joiner to make this joint.

Install the ridge beam. The ridge beam runs the length of the barn and provides support for the roof.

Attach the rafters to the ridge beam using metal hangers. This will help distribute the weight of the roof evenly.

Install the roof decking. You can use either plywood or OSB for this.

Install the roofing. You can use either metal roofing or shingles, depending on your preference.

Install the gable end trusses. These are the triangle-shaped frames that support the gable end of the barn.

Example: Let's say you want to build a barn with a 12' span and a pitch of 4/12. You would need to cut 8 2x8 rafters to a length of 13' 6". You would then cut a 4" notch in the bottom of each rafter, join the rafters using a scarf joint, and install the ridge beam. You would then attach the rafters to the ridge beam, install the roof decking, and finish by installing the roofing and gable end trusses.

GENERAL TECHNIQUE FOR SPACING RAFTERS

Rafter spacing refers to the distance between each rafter in a roof framing system. The correct spacing of rafters is important for several reasons, including:

Structural Integrity: Rafters that are spaced too far apart will not provide enough support to the roof deck and could lead to sagging or collapse. On the other hand, rafters that are spaced too close together will result in unnecessary material usage and increased costs.

Insulation: Proper rafter spacing is also important for ensuring adequate insulation in the roof cavity. Rafters that are spaced too closely together will reduce the amount of insulation that can be installed, which will negatively impact energy efficiency.

Ventilation: Proper rafter spacing is also important for ensuring adequate ventilation in the roof cavity. Rafters that are spaced too closely together will reduce the amount of ventilation that can be provided, which can lead to moisture buildup and other issues.

To determine the proper spacing of rafters, you will need to consider several factors, including the type of roofing material, the climate in which the building is located, building code requirements, and the type of insulation being used in the roof cavity.

Here is a general step-by-step guide to spacing rafters:

Determine the load requirements: The load requirements for the roof will dictate how closely the rafters must be spaced. This will depend on factors such as the type of roofing material, the climate, and the building code requirements for your area.

Choose the type of insulation: The type of insulation being used in the roof cavity will also impact the ideal rafter spacing. Certain types of insulation, such as blown-in insulation, will require more space than others.

Consider the type of roof: The type of roof being built will also impact the ideal rafter spacing. For example, a gable roof will have different requirements than a hip roof.

Check local building codes: Your local building codes will have specific requirements for rafter spacing, which must be followed.

Consult with a professional contractor or roofing expert: It is always a good idea to consult with a professional contractor or roofing expert to determine the ideal spacing for your specific roof design.

Once you have considered these factors, you can determine the ideal spacing for your rafters. A general rule of thumb is to space rafters at 16 to 24 inches on center (OC), but this will vary based on the specific requirements of your roof design.

HOW TO EFFICIENTLY CUT RIDGE BOARD, BIRDMOUTH,

AND TAIL END WHILE BUILDING RAFTERS

Cutting ridgeboard, birdmouth, and tail end accurately and efficiently is crucial to the success of a rafter building project. Here is a general step-by-step guide for cutting these components:

Ridgeboard: A ridgeboard, also known as a ridge beam, is a horizontal member that runs the length of the ridge of a roof and supports the rafters. To cut the ridgeboard, measure its length and mark the cut line with a square. Then, use a saw to cut.

Birdmouth: A birdmouth is a notch that is cut into the rafter to fit over the ridgeboard. To make the birdmouth, first measure and mark the location of the ridgeboard on the rafter. Then, use a framing square to mark the birdmouth cuts. Cut the birdmouth with a saw, making sure to cut at the right angle to ensure a tight fit with the ridgeboard.

Tail end: The tail end is the end of the rafter that extends beyond the wall plate. To cut the tail end, measure the length of the tail end required and mark the cut line with a square. Then, use a saw to cut.

To make the cuts efficiently, you should use a power saw such as a circular saw or miter saw, especially for large numbers of cuts. Additionally, a sharp saw blade will help ensure accurate and clean cuts.

It is important to measure and mark accurately to ensure that the ridgeboard, birdmouth, and tail end fit together properly. If you are not experienced in cutting these components, it may be best to consult with a professional contractor or roofing expert to ensure that the cuts are made correctly.

HOW TO INSTALL TRUSS RAFTERS

Installing truss rafters involves the following steps:

Preparation: Make sure you have all the necessary tools and materials, including trusses, hangers, brackets, fasteners, and a crane or hoisting equipment if necessary.

Layout: Measure and mark the location of the trusses on the wall plates, making sure they are level and spaced evenly apart.

Hanging: Use hangers or brackets to secure the trusses to the wall plates. The hangers or brackets should be attached to the wall plates and the trusses in the proper orientation.

Fastening: Use fasteners to secure the hangers or brackets to the wall plates and trusses. The type of fastener you use will depend on the material of the wall plates and trusses.

Bracing: Install bracing between the trusses to ensure stability and prevent them from moving. The bracing should be strong and securely fastened to the trusses.

Roofing: Once the trusses are securely installed, you can proceed with installing the roofing material, starting from the eave and working your way up.

It's important to follow the manufacturer's instructions and any local building codes and regulations when installing truss rafters. Consider hiring a professional if you're not confident in your ability to install truss rafters.

COMMON MISTAKES TO AVOID WHILE BUILDING RAFTERS AND HOW TO TROUBLESHOOT THEM

Building rafters requires accuracy and attention to detail to ensure that the roof structure is strong and secure. Here are some common mistakes to avoid and troubleshooting tips for each:

Incorrect measurement: One of the most common mistakes is an incorrect measurement, which can result in rafters that are too short or too long. To avoid this, measure and mark accurately, and double-check all measurements before making cuts.

Improper cutting: Another common mistake is improper cutting, such as cuts that are not at the correct angle or not deep enough. To avoid this, use a square to mark cuts, and make sure to use a saw with a sharp blade to ensure clean cuts.

Improper installation: Improper installation of hangers, ridgeboard or other components can cause problems with the roof structure. To avoid this, make sure to follow instructions carefully and check that each component is securely fastened.

Incorrect spacing: Incorrect spacing of rafters can result in weak spots in the roof structure. To avoid this, make sure to follow recommended spacing guidelines, and measure and mark each rafter before installing.

If you encounter problems with the roof structure, it is important to take corrective action as soon as possible to avoid further damage. In some cases, it may be necessary to seek the help of a professional contractor to repair or replace damaged components.

FAQ

Here are some common questions and answers about building rafters:

Q: What is a rafter in construction?

A: A rafter is a structural member in a roof that supports the roof deck and transfers the load of the roof to the walls of a building.

Q: What are the different types of rafters?

A: There are several types of rafters, including common rafters, hip rafters, jack rafters, valley rafters, and collar ties.

Q: How do you determine the size and design of a roof?

A: The size and design of a roof are determined by the size and shape of the building, the climate, and local building codes.

Q: What tools and materials are needed to build rafters?

A: Tools needed to build rafters include saws, hammers, nails, brackets, hangers, and measuring tape. Materials needed include lumber, roofing underlayment, and roofing materials.

Q: How do you determine the spacing of rafters?

A: The spacing of rafters is determined by the type of roof, the size of the building, and local building codes.

Q: What are some common mistakes to avoid when building rafters?

A: Common mistakes to avoid when building rafters include incorrect measurement, improper cutting, improper installation, and incorrect spacing.

Q: What should be done if there are problems with the roof structure?

A: If there are problems with the roof structure, it is important to take corrective action as soon as possible to avoid further damage. In some cases, it may be necessary to seek the help of a professional contractor to repair or replace damaged components.

CONCLUSION

In conclusion, building rafters for your roofing projects can be a rewarding and fulfilling experience. Not only does it give you the satisfaction of a job well done, but it can also save you money and ensure that your roof is built to last. Whether you are an experienced builder or a DIY enthusiast, with the right tools, materials, and guidance, anyone can learn to build strong and durable rafters. This book has provided a comprehensive guide to help you get started, and by following the steps outlined in these pages, you will be well on your way to becoming a confident and skilled rafter builder.

Remember, building rafters requires patience, attention to detail, and a willingness to learn. With each project, you will build your skills and knowledge, and you will be able to tackle increasingly complex roofing projects with confidence. So, don't be intimidated, grab your tools and materials, and get started on your rafter-building journey today!

THE END

Made in the USA
Las Vegas, NV
09 June 2024